30 Days to Increased Faith

Increase Your Faith, Attract God's Attention

And Achieve Your Dreams

RITA M. HENDERSON

Copyright © 2017 Rita M. Henderson Enterprises, L.L.C.

All rights reserved. reverendrita.org

ISBN-13: 978-1721936700

Dedication

To my maternal grandmother Kanzater Nadine Williams who loved me without pause and who believed in me when others didn't. I wish she were here now to share in the many experiences that I have had in Christ. I think she would be pleased with the Woman that I have become. I believe she stands on the balcony of witnesses cheering me on.

But without faith it is impossible to please him: for he that cometh to God must believe that he is, and that he is a rewarder of them that diligently seek him.

- Hebrews11:6KJV

Table of Contents

Introduction 1
Day 1 This Faith Works 1
Day 2 The Difference Is Clear 4
Day 3 Keeping the Faith Sure 6
Day 4 It Could Have Been You 8
Day 5 Going Through the Storm? 10
Day 6 Look Beyond the Storms 12
Day 7 Have You Compromised Your Faith? 14
Day 8 Not a Time for Discouragement 16
Day 9 Give, Even When It Is Difficult To 18
Day 10 Contend Earnestly For the Faith 20
Day 11 Stop Worrying: Weep Not, I Am Here 22
Day 12 God Shall Stand For You 24
Day 13 Authority of the Believer 26
Day 14 Have Dominion 28
Day 15 No Sword in David's Hand 30
Day 16 Early and Timely Satisfaction 32
Day 17 From The Miry Clay to Mountain Top 34
Day 18 Give Me This Mountain (Make a Demand) 36
Day 19 Changing With the Time 38
Day 20 Enduring Steadfastness 40
Day 21 Be Resilient, No Matter the Terrain 42
Day 22 It Is Not Time to Wash Your Nets 44

Day 23 Safeguard Your Good Name 46
Day 24 Triumphing Over Tragedies 48
Day 25 The Doors of Freedom 50
Day 26 Move Forward 52
Day 27 The Paths of Righteousness... 54
Day 28 A New and Better Beginning... 56
Day 29 Unlocking the Doors of Your Destiny 58
Day 30 Soar like The Eagle, Fly Eagle Fly 60
About the Author... 62

Introduction

Do not let this Book of law depart from your mouth; meditate on it, day and night (Joshua 1:8).

How else can we meditate on the Word? Reading the Bible may sometimes be simple and sometimes be difficult because of some confusing paradoxes, but with some more detailed explanations from books written by people under the inspiration of the Holy Spirit, then we can surely understand more.

Our human reasoning is way lower to understand the scriptures, but with prayer, Holy Spirit inspiration and faith, we would surely understand the scriptures, act the scriptures and live the scriptures.

Living the scriptures requires us to put our faith into action and this can be a very difficult thing. Faith is the substance of things hoped for, the evidence of things not seen (Hebrews 11:1). It's simply trusting in God despite the conditions and circumstances that you are facing. Let go and let God.

But without faith, it is impossible to please God; for he that cometh to God must believe that He is, and that He is a rewarder of them that diligently seek Him. Faith goes beyond what we can perceive with our physical senses; it does not work by the rules of science. Faith allows us to visibly and wholly believe in the invisible God that He can do anything for us inasmuch as we ask and we seek, we will find Him because He's always ready for us.

With this devotional you will learn more about the act of faith, how to put the faith into works and live the faith.

I pray that your lives be transformed and may you have series of testimonies afterward.

Thanks and God bless you.

Day 1
This Faith Works

But without faith it is impossible to please him: for he that cometh to God must believe that he is, and that he is a rewarder of them that diligently seek him.
- Hebrews 11:6

Dearly beloved, have faith in God. Faith is an essential part of our relationship with God. It is a prerequisite to beginning the conversion process, which is a necessary step on the road to salvation and eternal life. Now faith is the substance of things hoped for, the evidence of things not seen (Hebrews 11:1). Faith goes beyond what we can perceive with our physical senses, so it does not work by the rules of science. Faith allows us to believe that the invisible God can do what is physically impossible. In that sense, faith is built and grows on a spiritual plane, not a physical or scientific one. Read these profound scriptures : Jesus said, "For verily I say unto you, that whosoever shall say unto this mountain, Be thou removed, and be thou cast into the sea; and shall not doubt in his heart, but shall believe that those things which he saith shall come to pass; he shall have whatsoever he saith" (Mark 11:23). The book of Job affirms as follows: "Thou shalt also decree a thing, and it shall be established unto thee: and the light shall shine upon thy ways" (Job 22:28). Examples of men/women of faith: 1. Abraham: He believed God blindly: "And Abraham was a hundred years old when his son Isaac was born unto him" (Genesis 21:5). 2. Isaac: God instructed him to stay in a land infested with famine, he obeyed, and God prospered Him. "And the man waxed great, and went forward, and grew until he became very great" (Genesis 26:13). 3. Woman with the issue of blood: "For she said within herself, If I may but touch his garment, I shall be whole" (Matthew 9:21). 4. Apostle Paul: On the sail to Rome, faced with imminent shipwreck: "Wherefore, sirs, be of good cheer: for I believe God that it shall be even as it was told me" (Acts 27:25).

5. YOU: It is your turn! Have faith in God. It is done!

WHAT TO DO

1. Block your heart, mind and soul to unbelief and fear. Tell yourself in faith that "IT IS DONE!" 2. Ensure you are in good relationship with God, praise Him and make your request. Believe! 3. Confess and verbalize your faith until your joy is full, your loaded cloud will burst out with rain.

Prayer Points

- Father God, I believe, please help thou my unbelief.
- Father God, please speedily perform your counsel in my life, as I wait on you.
- Father God, please don't let me ever make a shipwreck of my faith.

In Jesus name, Amen

Day 2
The Difference Is Clear

I am crucified with Christ: nevertheless, I live; yet not I, but Christ liveth in me: and the life which I now live in the flesh I live by the faith of the Son of God, who loved me and gave himself for me.
- Galatians 2:20

Dear friend, a real Christian life is a life that is transparently clear to the onlookers. "Therefore if any man be in Christ, he is a new creature: old things are passed away; behold all things are become new" (2 Corinthians 5:17). Do a quick reflection of your Christian life; reflect about the quality of your life and its impacts on others. Is the difference clear? (Colossians 3:1-4). Check any relationship or association or any link whatsoever that will prevent you from making it to heaven; ask the Almighty God to destroy it today in Jesus name. All the little foxes and weights must go (Song of Solomon 2:15; Hebrews 12:1). Many of us have lost our first love for the Lord, and have been so preoccupied with worldly pursuits at the expense of our spiritual relationship with the Lord. Demas was a typical example: (2 Timothy 4:10). Another example was Lot's wife, her inability to severe her link with Sodom and Gomorrah cost her life (Genesis 19:26). God is pleading with you today; He is a God of another chance, come to Him now. "Even from the days of your fathers ye are gone away from mine ordinances and have not kept them. Return unto me, and I will return unto you, saith the Lord of hosts. But ye said wherein shall we return?" (Malachi 3:7). Yes, you can return!

WHAT TO DO

1. Return to your first love (Revelation 2:4-5). 2. Burn the bridge, no more looking back (Hebrew 10:38). 3. Be transformed by the renewal of your mind (Romans 12:2). 4. Get committed to the Lord

and His Word, and be busy with evangelism and soul winning (Matthew 28:19-20; Acts 1:8). 5. Engage in a life of daily examination and repositioning (2 Corinthians 13:5).

Prayer Points

- Father God, thank you for the opportunity to think over my life and faith in you.

- Father God, create in me a clean heart and renew a right spirit within me.

- Father God, restore unto me the joy of salvation and restore back my first love for you.

- Father God of another chance please let me never disappoint you again, no matter the pressure.

- Father God, please don't forsake me nor write me off but let me make it at last to heaven.

In Jesus name, Amen

Day 3
Keeping the Faith Sure

Let us hold fast the profession of our faith without wavering; for he is faithful that promised;
- Hebrews 10:23

Dearly beloved, there is the urgent need of keeping the faith. Glaringly, it seems we are living in an age where many are departing from the faith that was given to them. We as believers must be vigilant to be on guard not only to grow in the knowledge, word, and faith in Christ but to keep that which we received. The devil continues to try to steal, kill and destroy, but we must remember we are over comers in Christ (John 10:10). Apostle Paul was a typical example of someone who kept the faith till the very end. 1. "I have fought a good fight, I have finished my course, I have kept the faith: (2 Timothy 4:7)." 2. "Let us hold fast the profession of our faith without wavering; (for he is faithful that promised); (Hebrews 10:23)." 3. "Confirming the souls of the disciples, and exhorting them to continue in the faith, and that we must through much tribulation enter into the kingdom of God (Acts 14:22)." 4. "Therefore, my beloved brethren, be ye steadfast, unmovable, always abounding in the work of the Lord, forasmuch as ye know that your labour is not in vain in the Lord (1 Corinthians 15:58)." 5. "Looking unto Jesus the author and finisher of our faith; who for the joy that was set before him endured the cross, despising the shame, and is set down at the right hand of the throne of God (Hebrews 12:2)." Some hindrances to steadfastness in faith: 1. Fear and doubt 2. Worldliness and sinful habits 3.Prayerlessness 4.Keeping bad friends and company 5. Not enduring sound doctrine.

WHAT TO DO

1. We should all desire in our lives to one day hear Him say, well done good and faithful servant. 2. We need to live daily in our faith not just

on Sunday or midweek. 3. Regular devotions, prayer and reading the Word should be part of our daily faith walk. 4. We must be doers of the Word and never give up. (1 Corinthians 16:13) 5. Let the world see our faith through the Christian works of faith in our daily living.

Prayer Points

- Father God, may every pillar of fear and doubt that has been sowed into my life be dismantled.

- Father God, let my faith work for me in my circumstances.

- Father God, let my faith and expressions thereof be attractive forces for men to know you.

- Father God, by your mighty power, clear from my pathway every mountain and obstacle.

- Father God, let my faith in you lead me on till I see you in glory.

In Jesus name, Amen

Day 4
It Could Have Been You

"Brethren, if a man be overtaken in a fault, ye which are spiritual, restore such an one in the spirit of meekness; considering thyself, lest thou also be tempted."
- Galatians 6:1

Most of us who stumbled at one time or the other in this Christian race would have said "That can never happen to me" Really! We are all kept by God's mercy and power (1 Peter 1:5; Ephesians 2:8). Dear, we have a command to and responsibility to restore those who err regardless of the nature of the transgression. How do we do this? 1. Help them to acknowledge their sins (Psalms 51:4). 2. Help them in love to accept responsibility for the consequences of their misdeeds. 3. Pray genuinely with them to repent, and completely turn away from such paths. 4. Rebuild and encourage their confidence in the Lord through fellowship. 5. Let them also be helpers in the faith of those who might fall into such errors in the future. We have several examples of brethren restoring weaker ones in the Bible: 1. David: David restored Mephibosheth grandson of Saul to the path of royal prosperity (2 Samuel 9:9-11). 2. Peter: Having denied the Lord despite his boastings, Jesus restored him (John 21:15-17). 3. Paul: After threatening and persecuting early Christians, God arrested him, and he needed to be encouraged and disciple, Ananias was used to help him (Acts 9:17-21).

WHAT TO DO

1. Don't think you cannot fall, pray for grace to remain steadfast (1 Corinthians 10:12). 2. Never rejoice over a falling brother, but bring such up for we are helpers of each other's in faith (2 Corinthians 1:24). 3. Let us encourage deep and sincere fellowship (Hebrews 10:25).

Prayer Points

- Father God, you are my hope and rock, please keep me from falling.

- Father God the grace to bear other's burdens let it come upon me.

- Father God, deliver me from the power of the devil and please strengthen my faith.

- Father God, please help me to humble myself and not to think of myself more highly than I should.

In Jesus name, Amen

Day 5
Going Through the Storm?

When thou passest through the waters, I will be with thee; and through the rivers, they shall not overflow thee: when thou walkest through the fire, thou shalt not be burned; neither shall the flame kindle upon thee.
- Isaiah 43:2

"I don't understand what is happening again! I pay my tithe regularly, and perform my functions as a true soldier of Christ." Dearly beloved, I feel for you and can understand where you are coming from. Many genuine children of God have passed through that way before also. There are times when our hearts are overwhelmed, and it seems the ground is caving in on us (Psalm 61:2, Psalms 77:3, Psalms 143:4). Hear what Job said "If a man dies shall he live again? All the days of my appointed time will I wait, till my change come" (Job 14:14). Examples of those who were severely overwhelmed with challenges of life and they overcame: 1. Joseph: He was hated by his blood brothers, sold into slavery, suffered harassment in Potiphar's house, ended up in prison, but God turned his misery to great fortune as a Prime Minister in a strange land (Genesis 37, Genesis 39, Genesis 41). 2. Job: A very righteous man that feared the Lord, suffered unprecedentedly sorrow and was stripped of every possession, God preserved him and made his latter end very glorious (Job 1, Job 42). 3. David: Very young and innocent, poor shepherd boy was anointed to take over from King Saul, who left his throne to haunt this poor lad; who was thoroughly overwhelmed with shadows of death. God delivered David from destruction and made him king despite all the evil plans of King Saul (1 Samuel 16:12, 1 Samuel 19:1). 4. YOU: Men have treated you badly, rode on your back and still hate you; don't despair, God will also come through for you (Psalms 66:12).

WHAT TO DO

1. In your desperate situation, call on the Lord for safety and deliverance (Psalms 71:20). 2. Reject any solutions from the Kingdom of darkness (Ephesians 5:11). 3. Stay and focus on God alone (Hebrews 12:2).

Prayer Points

- Father God, thank you for giving me hope, please hold me close and deliver me.

- Father God, when my heart is overwhelmed, please take me to the rock that is higher than I.

- Father God, let me rejoice in you no matter what happens around me; I will wait till my change comes.

- Father God, please let goodness and mercy follow me as I wait patiently for your swift intervention in my specific situation.

In Jesus name, Amen

Day 6
Look Beyond the Storms

Yea, though I walk through the valley of the shadow of death, I will fear no evil: for thou art with me; thy rod and thy staff they comfort me.
- Psalms 23:4

Storms as much as they could be disastrous and frightening are in most cases propellers of destiny for children of God (Romans 8:28). In the attainment and fulfillment of purpose in life, we sometimes have to go through very stormy challenges occasioned by circumstances and even forces beyond us. Many heroes looked beyond the storm; for the storm is for a while, sooner or later the storm will be over, and calmness will return. "For his anger endureth but a moment; in his favour is life: weeping may endure for a night, but joy cometh in the morning" (Psalms 30:5). In the book of Job, we learned some lessons about ways of handling storm: Here we go: 1. God knows about the storm even before it starts (Job 1:8-12; Acts 15:18). 2. Your response or confession to the storm to a large extent dictates the consequences of the storm (Job 19:25). 3. God has the capacity and capability to silence every storm no matter how fierce (Mark 4:35-41; Job 42:10). 4. The presence of God in the storm is absolutely uncompromisable (Job 42:1-2; Genesis 39:21). 5. Storms are stepping stones to higher glory. Examples are: - Joseph in Egypt: His trials led to triumph (Genesis 41:44), David at Ziklag: His faith in God, personal encouragement, and determination paid off (1 Samuel 30:6), Esther at Shushan Palace: By her actions, the Jews defeated their enemies (Esther 8:17), Paul on the way to Rome: God's presence sustained him through the storm (Acts 27:22-25).

WHAT TO DO

1. Fear not, Jesus is with you. 2. Focus on Jesus only you won't sink. 3. Fervently put your faith in God who can still the storm.

Prayer Points

➢ Father God, unto Thee, do I lift my eyes, please be the shelter in times of storms.

➢ Father God let me ride higher on the wings of the storm into my destiny.

➢ Father God, in every storm of life, let me reach the shore safely and in joy.

In Jesus Name, Amen

Rita M. Henderson

Day 7
Have You Compromised Your Faith?

Nebuchadnezzar spake and said unto them, Is it true, O Shadrach, Meshach, and Abed–nego, do not ye serve my gods, nor worship the golden image which I have set up?
- Daniel 3:14

Dearly beloved, when you are faced with the reality of choosing between Godly principles and highly intimidating offers from kings and people, what should be your response? Some children of God are falling like packs of cards because of worldly pursuits and the economic meltdown. What is your character made of? Can you have a purpose firm like the three Hebrew children and Daniel? (Matthew 6:33). "Then Peter and the other apostles answered and said we ought to obey God rather than men" (Acts 5:29). "But Daniel purposed in his heart that he would not defile himself with the portion of the king's meat, nor with the wine which he drank: therefore he requested of the prince of the eunuchs that he might not defile himself"(Daniel1:8). Why do some easily compromise? 1. Fear of losing favour and opportunities with the kings and influential people, Peter rebuked by Paul (Galatians 2:11-12). 2. Fear of intimidation and harassment. For example, Harassment of Nehemiah (Nehemiah 2:19). 3. Fear of being tagged a "wet blanket" by people.
e.g. King Saul (1 Samuel 15:21-23). 4. Fear of persecution: (2 Timothy 1:8). 5. Fear of being "cast out" amidst friends or company of others e.g. Parent of a man born blind (John 9:19-22).

WHAT TO DO

1. Be ye separate, touch not the unclean thing. 2. Be personally determined to go all the way for the Saviour. 3. Trust more in the Lord

than in princes. 4. Let His Word be your guide daily. 5. Watch and pray without ceasing.

Prayer Points

- ➤ Father God, thank you for another day in the land of the living.

- ➤ Father God, I lay down all my "idols" and "thrones" I have made, that has taken my heart. Please cleanse me thoroughly.

- ➤ Father God, send divine help, give me boldness and grace to say no when the situation goes against my faith in you.

- ➤ Father God let my soul find fulfillment and expression in your voice and not of men.

In Jesus name, Amen

Day 8
Not a Time for Discouragement

And David was greatly distressed; for the people spake of stoning him, because the soul of all the people was grieved, every man for his sons and for his daughters: but David encouraged himself in the Lord his God.
- 1 Samuel 30:6

Dearly beloved, events all over the world in recent times are enough to discourage even the Lion hearted. Disappointments and discouragements are tools bringing fear that dampens our faith. This is the ploy of the enemy, and we must not fall for it at all. Are you in despair, unsure of what tomorrow holds, discouraged from the front, left, right and center? Don't give up! Encourage yourself in the Lord our God, He will see you through. You must develop a tough skin. Shifting your focus from the Lord is the foundation for discouragement and frustrations (Hebrews 12:2). Examples: 1. Elijah: A powerful and fearless prophet of God got discouraged at life because of a threat from Queen Jezebel. "But he went a day's journey into the wilderness, and came and sat down under a juniper tree: and he requested for himself that he might die; and said, it is enough; now, O Lord, take away my life; for I am not better than my fathers." God sent His Angel to minister to Elijah (1 Kings 19:4). 2. David: He was so discouraged, but he called on the Lord and encouraged himself in the Lord his God, and there was a positive change of his situation (1 Samuel 30:6-8, 1 Samuel 30:18-19). God further says: 1. "Say to them that are of a fearful heart, be strong, fear not: behold, your God will come with vengeance, even God with a recompense; he will come and save you" (Isaiah 35:4 2). "And he answered, Fear not: for they that be with us are more than they that be with them" (2 Kings 6:16). 3. "For I the Lord thy God will hold thy right hand, saying unto thee, Fear not; I will help thee" (Isaiah 41:13).

WHAT TO DO

1. Fear not, call on the Lord, He will answer. 2. Confront all the Pharaohs, Goliaths, etc. in the name of the Lord. 3. Ask the Lord for direction and strategies. 4. Use the WORD OF GOD and speak to the situations while you maintain your peace.

Prayer Points

- Father God, look around me, my courage is failing, please hold my hand and encourage me.

- Father God, when no other help is near, the help of the helpless please stand by me.

- Father God, the world, and situations might change, but not You; You will never; Thou who changeth not, please abide with me.

- Father God, let me pursue, overtake and recover all; it is my turn to be blessed.

In Jesus Name, Amen

Day 9
Give, Even When It Is Difficult To

Give, and it shall be given unto you; good measure, pressed down, shaken together, running over, shall men give to your bosom. - Luke 6:38a.

Dearly beloved, we are living in a season that is so difficult to give, but this is the time God expects us to sacrificially and joyfully. The way out of lack is simply by giving. There are basic principles in the word of God which when applied correctly give precise results. God is a God of principles, and will not break His laws, but at the same time, He is no respecter of persons. Many children of God are struggling with poverty or lack because they are stingy, and they think they are wise (Proverbs 3:7). Some sow on unproductive soil and have no returns on their giving. You must give and sow your life out of lack and poverty. Examples of givers: 1. God the Father gave His only begotten son (John 3:16). 2. Jesus, He freely offered His own life. 3. Abraham: Did not spare Isaac, the promised child. What are some principles of giving: 1. Don't rob God in tithes and offerings (Malachi 3:10). 2. God is the supplier of all things (Psalms 24:1). 3. Give bountifully to God and fellow humans. 4. Giving must be sacrificial (John 3:16; Rom.8:32). 5. Giving must be done cheerfully (2 Cor.9:7). 6. When you give, it will come back to you (Eccl. 11:1). 5. Due to the law of harvest, as you give, God will make men give to you. 6. Givers never lack, stingy people tend towards poverty (Proverbs 11:24). 7. What you give to others, you get back in multiple folds (Luke 6:38b).

WHAT TO DO

1. Stop being stingy; there is nothing you have that God has not given you (2 Corinthians 9:8). 2. Be an unrepentant and cheerful giver (2

Corinthians 9:7). 3. Give sacrificially, sow even in hard times (Psalms 126:5; Genesis 26:12-13).

Prayer Points

- Father God, thank you for reminding me that all good things come from you; I am grateful.

- Father God, purge every tendency to be stingy, egocentric, selfish and uncaring from my life.

- Father God, please give me a heart that gives cheerfully and sacrificially.

- Father God, please don't let all my sowings be in vain; remember my offerings and sacrifice.

In Jesus Name, Amen

Day 10
Contend Earnestly For the Faith

Beloved, when I gave all diligence to write unto you of the common salvation, it was needful for me to write unto you, and exhort you that ye should earnestly contend for the faith which was once delivered unto the saints.
- Jude 1:3

Dearly beloved, do you realize how these days you easily overlook some areas of your life you held so dear before; how innocently the thought "it doesn't matter" now becomes a daily part of your life? Watch out! (1 Peter 5:8-9). Here is a list of few of the "it doesn't matter's": 1. Spending long hours on trivialities and vanities of life (Ecclesiastes 2:17). 2. Not enduring the hard truth of the Word, but always interested in "quick fix" (2 Timothy 4:3). 3. Preferring clubs, watching football, going partying, etc. to having fellowship with the brethren (Hebrews 10:25). 4. Trivializing lies and falsehood (Proverbs 20:23). Examples: 1. Samson: took his anointing casually and paid dearly for it (Judges 14:3; 16:19-21). 2. Esau: Hunger gave way to deprivation and loss of destiny (Genesis 25:32; Genesis 27:34). 3. Demas: Colleague of Luke and Mark made a shipwreck of his faith (Philemon 1:24; 2 Tim.4:10).

WHAT TO DO

1. Run for cover, flee all demonic influence (1 Timothy 6:10-11). 2. Keep looking at the perfect law of liberty (James 1:25). 3. Be violent with the devil (Matthew 11:12). 4. Banish fear and harassment from satanic agents and haters of Jesus Christ (Galatians 5:1).

Prayer Points

➢ Father God, don't let me make a shipwreck of my faith.

➢ Father God, give me boldness against satanic manipulations and of darkness.

➢ Father God, let my faith endure till the end.

In Jesus Name, Amen

Rita M. Henderson

Day 11
Stop Worrying: Weep Not, I Am Here

And when the Lord saw her, he had compassion on her, and said unto her, weep not.
- Luke 7:13.

Dearly beloved, our Lord Jesus Christ promised to be with us no matter the situation we go through in life. He knows the way through the wilderness; stop worrying. He is right here now to assist you. For example in Luke 7:11-16, a widow was bereaved of her only son. Her only hope had been dashed. Mourners followed her, but that was the best they could do. Her wall collapsed, and her world thinned out. She wept until her voice could hardly be heard. Are you holding on to the last straw in your marriage, finance, business, ministry or personal life? Jesus is in the business of showing compassion; He says to you "weep not," no more tears (Psalms 30:5). God can still raise the dead bones of your situation as you prophesy (Ezekiel 37:10). Dead trees at the smell of water can still sprout to life and bud again (Job 14:7-9). There is still hope for you to be what God ordained you to be. Don't give up and be down cast. God will raise you up again. Wipe away the tears; no more tears! Your sun will shine again. God will make a way for you (Isaiah 43:20). The Bible is full of examples of people God wiped away their sorrows and tears. He is no respecter of persons, and He will do yours.

WHAT TO DO

1. Go back, in absolute surrender to Him; He is waiting to show you compassion (Psalms 102:13). 2. People will sympathize or even empathize with your situation; they raptly listen to your full story but, Jesus is not interested in your failure, but He offers compassion.

Take it! 3. Believe and confess that He can make your dark clouds to disappear, and bring you a brighter and sunny day. 4. Prophesy into your life, family, marriage, business, country, and ministry. Receive mercy, peace, and joy today.

Prayer Points

- ➢ Father God, arise and have mercy on me; show me your compassion.

- ➢ Father God, men can sympathize, but you can bring life. Jesus, please speak life into me and all my realms today.

- ➢ Father God, please step boldly into the matters of my life and restore joy in Jesus name.

- ➢ Father God, turn everything that makes me weep into joy and laughter.

- ➢ Father God, let my life take a new dimension of greatness from today in Jesus.

- ➢ Father God, fill my life with joy unspeakable and let me serve you better.

In Jesus Name, Amen

Rita M. Henderson

Day 12
God Shall Stand For You

For I know that my redeemer liveth, and that he shall stand at the latter day upon the earth:
- Job 19:25

The best thing that can happen in the life of a child of God is the assurance that God lives in us, and His presence goes with us, and so He will stand for us in the long run, no matter how hard the times and the circumstances (Psalms 30:5). No one ever desires to go through the kind of trial Job went through. In the conflicting suggestions by the wife and his three friends, He remained resolute and unshakable in the Lord his God just like David (1 Samuel 30:18). God will stand for you today; this is your season of grace and favor (Psalms 102:13). God is shielding you from evil and replacing your shame with glory, and is lifting up your head (Psalms 3:3). Examples: 1. Joseph: And God was with Joseph (Acts 7:9, Genesis 39:2-3, Genesis 39:21 & Genesis 39-23). 2. David: The Lord of hosts was his Ally (2 Samuel 5:10, 1 Samuel 18:28). 3. Stephen: He beheld Jesus in His glory (Acts 7:55-56). 4. Daniel: God's presence was with him in the Lions' den (Daniel 6:23). 5. YOU: Jesus will not leave you, will not forsake you, and will not abandon you (Hebrews 13:5, Deuteronomy 31:6).

WHAT TO DO

1. Acquaint yourself with God (Job 22:21). 2. Obey Him completely (Isaiah 1:19). 3. Honour Him, so that He can honour you (1 Samuel 2:30b). 4. Let God create in you a new heart. (Psalms 51:10-12).

Prayer Points

- Father God, please don't let your presence depart from me.

- Father God as I pass through this pilgrim's way, be thou my guide.

- Father God, I cannot do without you, please do not forsake nor abandon me.

- Father God, please prosper and take me to the top, no matter how tough is the terrain.

In Jesus Name, Amen

Rita M. Henderson

Day 13
Authority of the Believer

Thou shalt make thy prayer unto him, and he shall hear thee, and thou shalt pay thy vows. Thou shalt also decree a thing, and it shall be established unto thee: and the light shall shine upon thy ways.
- Job 22:27-28

Dearly beloved friends, do you know you have tremendous power in your mouth as a believer, and as a child of the Most High God? There is so much power in your tongue, strong enough to save lives or kill. You can command things to happen, and God will back you up if you comply with His Word. "Death and life are in the power of the tongue: and they that love it shall eat the fruit thereof"
(Proverbs 18:21). Hear the Lord Jesus Himself: "For verily I say unto you, That whosoever shall say unto this mountain, Be thou removed, and be thou cast into the sea; and shall not doubt in his heart, but shall believe that those things which he saith shall come to pass; he shall have whatsoever he saith" (Mark 11:23). Your mouth is the avenue through which your faith is expressed for the elements and spirits to hear and respond appropriately. Examples of those who decreed in the Bible: 1. Elijah: Decreed dryness and rain in the space of three and a half years (James 5:17-18). 2. Elisha: Decreed leprosy to the lineage of Gehazi for ever (2 Kings 5:27). 3. Samuel: Decreed an end to the reign of King Saul, and got David anointed (1 Samuel 15:28). 4. Paul: Decreed blindness on Elymas, the sorcerer (Acts 13:11).

WHAT TO DO

To do list: Elements of establishing a decree. 1. Know who you are in the Lord (1 Peter 2:9). 2. Hold fast the Word of life (Philippians. 2:16). 3. Have absolute and unshaken faith in God (Hebrews 11:6). 4. Verbalize your desires and requests in prayer and deep communion with God (Mark 11:23). 5. Be expectant to see the manifestation of your requests (Proverbs 23:18). 6. While waiting, be full of worship & praise (Psalms 34:1).

Prayer Points

Father God, thank You for giving me prophetic utterance, I decree in the name of Jesus Christ that: (a). Every counsel of the enemy concerning me and my household is hereby annulled. (b). Every desire of my heart shall be granted as I exercise my faith in the Lord Jesus Christ. (c). Whatsoever I lay my hands on henceforth shall prosper and multiply. (d). Every evil plan concerning Our country shall be scattered and destroyed. (e). I shall be light to the Gentiles, and salt to the earth. (f). My tomorrow shall be alright and glorious, and I shall reach the top.

In Jesus Name, Amen

Day 14
Have Dominion

Behold, thou shalt call a nation that thou knowest not, and nations that knew not thee shall run unto thee because of the Lord thy God, and for the Holy One of Israel; for he hath glorified thee.
- Isaiah 55:5

Dear brethren, today's menu is to remind us once again that God intends that our influence and control should go beyond our local environment. You must be in dominion and affect Nations (Genesis 1:28). Nations of the world will beckon on you, and you will venture into strange lands and be blessed. Remember even in the preaching of the gospel; the Lord commands us to go to the uttermost parts of the earth (Acts 1:8). No matter your calling and profession, you will go places for Jesus and men will favour you, and the glory of the Lord will shine around you (Isaiah 60:1-3). Examples: 1. Isaac: This man prospered so much that a whole nation envied him (Genesis 26:12-14). 2. Joseph: From servitude, became the Prime Minister over the nation that enslaved him (Genesis 41:31-44). 3. Esther: An orphan and a slave became a Queen over a vast kingdom (Esther 2:17). 4. Daniel: A captivity of Babylon became a lead counselor for kings of Babylon, and the third in position in the land (Daniel 5:29). 5. Paul: God made him to be an Apostle to the nations around Israel in his time (Romans 11:13). 6. You: Arise and take over and govern the nations and show forth God's glory and praise (1 Peter 2:9).

WHAT TO DO

1. Be willing to go anywhere He sends you. 2. Refuse to be a Jonah, don't run away. 3. Ask for the power of the Holy Spirit to operate beyond borders. 4. Seek to be a true and committed Ambassador of Christ indeed. 5. Don't be intimidated by the enemy.

Prayer Points

➤ Father God, thank You for choosing me to do Your will, please enable me to perform.

➤ Father God In the mighty name of Jesus, I break every barrier obstructing my reaching out and enlarging my territory and coast.

➤ Father God, take me to Nations, and let them come to the brightness of Your glory in my life.

➤ Father God, let my children and generations following have great, positive and mighty influence over nations of the earth.

➤ Father God, darkness can never overcome light, please let the church in our Nation rise above obscurity.

In Jesus Name, Amen

Rita M. Henderson

Day 15
No Sword in David's Hand

So David prevailed over the Philistine with a sling and with a stone, and smote the Philistine, and slew him, but there was no sword in the hand of David.
- 1 Samuel 17:50

In this world, so long as we interact with others; we will always face battles. The interesting thing, however, is that no matter how fierce the battle, we will always be victorious (Romans 8:37, 2 Corinthians 2:14). The battle can be related to health, finance, marriage, business or even ministry. With God, we can win a battle without a fight. Has it not occurred to you that in the battles of life, the real Warrior is God Himself and only using you as a physical symbol to deal with the enemy? (a). "The Lord shall fight for you, and ye shall hold your peace" (Exodus 14:14). (b). Be not afraid nor dismayed by reason of this great multitude; for the battle is not yours, but God's" (2 Chronicles 20:15). (c). "Some trust in chariots, and some in horses: but we will remember the name of the Lord our God" (Psalms 20:7). (d). "With him is an arm of flesh; but with us is the Lord our God to help us and to fight our battles" (2 Chronicles 32:8). Example of David: (1 Samuel 17:17-58) 1. He never had any military training, though his brothers were in the military. 2. God gave him natural training with the Lion, and with the Bear in the bush. 3. He never had any conventional weapon but just a sling and stone. 4. He was more interested in using God's name than in King Saul's armor. 5. He was ready to confront Goliath headlong, while others were dodging.

WHAT TO DO

1. Depend absolutely on the Lord (Psalms 124:8). 2. Do not be afraid of the enemy (Jeremiah 1:8). 3. Don't be discouraged by others

(Isaiah 50:7). 4. Take your instruction from the Lord and go in His name (Psalms 60:12).

Prayer Points

- ➤ Father God, no matter the battles before me, please fight for me.

- ➤ Almighty God, you are the Master Strategist, teach my hands to do valiantly.

- ➤ Father God, help me not to rely on the arm of flesh so that I don't become a victim.

In Jesus Name, Amen

Rita M. Henderson

Day 16
Early and Timely Satisfaction

O satisfy us early with thy mercy; that we may rejoice and be glad all our days.
- Psalms 90:14

Dearly beloved, as we all know and understand, manufacturers of products or providers of services must satisfy the market to keep being relevant in today's world. The earlier your consumers are satisfied with your products or services, the more likely the continuous patronage. Examples of those with very early blessings: 1. Josiah: He started reigning at the age of eight (2 Chronicles 34:1). 2. David: He was a teenager when he was anointed King of Israel (1 Samuel 16:11-12). 3. Samuel: He was given as a gift to the Lord at a very tender age, and God used him mightily (1 Samuel 1:24-28). 4. Solomon: God blessed him tremendously while he's very young on the throne of his father David (1 Chronicles 29:1). Further lessons: 1. God is our Manufacturer (Creator), and our service Provider (Genesis 1:28; Philippians 4:19). 2. He has made adequate provisions for us (1 Peter 1:3; Romans 8:32; Ephesians 3:20). 3. He is willing to satisfy our needs upon request. Ask, and you shall be given, Seek, and you shall find, Knock, and it shall be opened unto you (Matthew 7:7). 4. Many people ask when it is almost too late; for you to enjoy maximum benefits, you must ask early enough. Those who seek me early shall find me (Proverbs 8:17). For you, are things always getting late or totally exhausted when it gets to your turn, leading to fear, sorrow, unfulfilled dreams or depression? God has answers waiting for you, to make your joy full (John 16:24).

WHAT TO DO

1. Place an early order or demand on your request to the Lord (Psalms 5:3). 2. Ask bountifully; ask UNTIL your joy is FULL (John

16:24). 3. Step out in faith and doubt not (Mark 11:22-24). 4. Praise Him ahead of the blessings (Psalms 34:1). 5. Do not ask amiss (James 4:3).

Prayer Points

- Father God, thank You for a new day, I bless and glorify Your Holy name.

- Father God, I have come again, please speedily hear me out, time is going, urgently help me, my Lord.

- Father God, satisfy me early with Your mercy; don't let age catch up on me, let me rejoice and be glad all my days.

- Father God, if You don't do it quickly, they will laugh me to scorn and say "where is now thy God?"

- Father God, help me to pursue, overtake, and recover all missed opportunities.

- Father God, You are my shield and glory, please wipe away my shame and frustration.

- Father God, please grant me divine speed and mercy, Thou the lifter up of mine head.

In Jesus Name, Amen

Day 17
From The Miry Clay to Mountain Top

He brought me up also out of a horrible pit, out of the miry clay, and set my feet upon a rock, and established my goings.
- Psalms 40:2

Please! Please!! Please!!! Stop thinking that way! You are not the worst person on earth. God can raise anybody from the worst situation to the best position possible (Jeremiah 32:17). The Lord is set to lift you up; it doesn't matter for how long you have been denied your rightful possession. "He raiseth up the poor out of the dust, and lifteth up the beggar from the dunghill, to set them among princes, and to make them inherit the throne of glory: for the pillars of the earth are the Lord's, and he hath set the world upon them" (1 Samuel 2:8). Examples: If God can bring water out of the rock then your case is not hopeless (Numbers 20:8). If the barren Sarah, overripped with menopause can have a child, your case is not hopeless (Genesis 21:6-8). If an orphan slave young Lady, Esther can be Miss World and later a Queen, your case is not hopeless (Esther 2:17). If a forgotten and cursed person, Jabez can be blessed above his fellows then your case is not hopeless (1 Chronicles 4:9-10). If a multidemon possessed harlot, Mary Magdalene can become a trusted follower of Jesus, then your case is not hopeless (Luke 8:2). If a forsaken fugitive grandson of Saul, Mephibosheth could be favoured to have the family's Estate and to eat continually at King David's table, then your case is not hopeless (2 Samuel 9:7).

WHAT TO DO

1. Call upon the Lord; He is waiting to answer you (Jeremiah 33:3).
2. Have genuine faith in Him and seek Him diligently (Hebrews 11:6).

3. Trust Him to do the impossible no matter what the challenge is (Psalms 37:5). 4. Ask for His mercy (Romans 9:15-16).

Prayer Points

- Father God, lift me up from the miry clay of life and position me on the mountain of peace, joy, favour and abundance.

- Father God, with you it is never too late, please grant divine speed to settle my peculiar case.

- Father God, when it is well with me, don't let me deny your love and forget you; establish my going.

- Father God, please sustain me at the top, don't let me become an Ex-Champion.

In Jesus Name, Amen

Day 18
Give Me This Mountain (Make a Demand)

Now, therefore give me this mountain, whereof the Lord spake in that day; for thou in that day how the Anakims were there, and that the cities were great and fenced: if so be the Lord will be with me, then I shall be able to drive them out, as the Lord said.
- Joshua 14:12

Caleb was a colleague of Joshua who gave positive reports concerning Israel's ability to conquer their gigantic enemies. Moses, the servant of God had earlier promised that inheritance to Caleb. It is very instructive that Caleb held unto the promise and eventually got it after 45 years. Have you been waiting for the fulfillment of a particular Word or promise of God in your life, and it seems like a mirage? Do not keep quiet, make a demand for it like Caleb did. Here are reasons why you must do so: 1. God is not a liar, what He promised, He will fulfill (Numbers 23:19). 2. His plans for you are great and fantastic (Jeremiah 29:11). 3. He answers prayer (Matthew 7:7; Jeremiah 33:3). 4. He delights in your prosperity (Psalms 35:27).
5. All things are yours to enjoy (Matthew 6:33).

WHAT TO DO

1. Remind Him of His Word and promises to you (2 Corinthians 1:20). 2. Praise and Worship Him, that's the best method to make Him fight for you (2 Chronicles 20:21-24). 3. Please Him in every way (Proverbs 3:5-6). 4. Be bold, courageous and do exploits against the enemies of God as Caleb did (Numbers 13:30; Daniel 11:32b). 5. Love what He loves, and hate what He hates (Proverbs 8:17, Hebrews 1:9).

Prayer Points

- Father God, remember your wonderful promises to me, please bring them to pass.

- Father God, please make haste to help me, I need divine acceleration.

- Father God, no matter what it takes, let my destiny be actualized early enough in my life.

- Father God, help me to honour you daily in all aspects of my life.

In Jesus Name, Amen

Day 19
Changing With the Time

Nevertheless, the foundation of God standeth sure, having this seal, The Lord knoweth them that are his. And, Let every one that nameth the name of Christ depart from iniquity.
- 2 Timothy 2:19

Dearly beloved, compromise is one great stumbling block the children of God are confronted with in this our generation, and it makes us bend the rules, cut corners and at times, outrightly violate the very principles and values we once believed in and wholly cherished. In this rapidly changing world, don't let the world change your mind. It hurts God so much. "And be not conformed to this world: but be ye transformed by the renewing of your mind, that ye may prove what is that good, and acceptable, and perfect, will of God" (Romans 12:2). Changing with the world in our desires, speech, dressing, conduct, behavior, likes and dislikes goes beyond our outward indicators; it shows what is deeply seated on our inside. "For as he thinketh in his heart, so is he" (Proverbs 23:7a.). "For out of the abundance of the heart the mouth speaketh" (Matthew 12:34b). "Can the fig tree, my brethren, bear olive berries? Either a vine, figs?so can no fountain both yield salt water and fresh" (James 3:12). Examples of those who refused to compromise: 1. Joseph: Had it all in Potiphar's house but maintained his integrity in the Lord (Genesis 39:9). 2. Daniel: He chose not to defile Himself with the King's portions (Daniel 1:8). 3. Jesus: Our Master and perfect example, refused to bow to the devil (Matthew 4:1-11). 4. YOU: Take a firm stand for Jesus today (Hebrews 3:15).

WHAT TO DO

1. Hold on to God, and do according to his Word (Psalms 119:11). 2. Abstain from all appearance of evil (1 Thessalonians 5:22).

3. Submit to God and resist the devil (James 4:7). 4. Be vigilant and pray (1 Peter 5:8-9).

Prayer Points

- ➤ Father God, I need Your grace to stand up for Jesus, please help me.

- ➤ Father God, grant me boldness to resist any advance from the devil.

- ➤ Father God, let Your Word continually transform my life till Your image is perfected in me.

- ➤ Father God, in my life, dear Lord, please do not let my pilgrimage here on earth be a waste.

In Jesus Name, Amen

Day 20
Enduring Steadfastness

Therefore, my beloved brethren, be ye stedfast, unmovable, always abounding in the work of the Lord, forasmuch as ye know that your labour is not in vain in the Lord.
- 1 Corinthians 15:58

Dearly beloved, there is nothing God detests in our attitude to His work like lukewarmness or ambiguity (Revelation.3:15-16). God demands to know your stand; there is no room for instability. Unstable people cannot excel and cannot receive anything from the Lord (Genesis 49:4; James 1:6-8). Examples of unstable people: 1. Reuben (Genesis 49:3-4). 2. Children of Israel (1 Kings 18:21). 3. Christians (James 3:11). Examples of stable and focused people: 1. Daniel (Daniel 1:8). 2. Joseph (Genesis 39:9). 3. Job (Job 19:25).

WHAT TO DO

1. Repent and get focused (Acts 3:19). 2. Fix your gaze on Jesus (Hebrews 12:2). 3 .Have faith in God (Mark 11:22). 4. Be totally committed to His work (Mark 13:13).

Prayer Points

- ➤ Father God in Your mercy, please stabilize me, and keep me focused.

- ➤ Father God, anything that will make me lukewarm, please take away.

- ➤ Father God please increase my faith in Your Word and let me do exploits.

➢ Father God, please don't let me labour in vain, after all said and done, let me make heaven at last.

    In Jesus Name, Amen

Rita M. Henderson

Day 21
Be Resilient, No Matter the Terrain

Now the just shall live by faith: but if any man draw back, my soul shall have no pleasure in him.
- Hebrew 10:38

Dearly beloved, this Christian journey is a one-way traffic, there is no diversion or going backward; doing so will be a violation of the rules, and the consequences are not desirable at all (Genesis 19:26). In the weapons provided for us, no provision was made for the back because we are expected to keep moving forward till all the enemies are vanquished (Ephesians 6:13-17). Jesus said once you put your hands on the plough there is no looking back (Luke 9:62). Are you tired of this journey, considering others with their lands and gold, and you wonder what is happening to you? Keep your focus, don't be discouraged; God will come through for you as you keep gazing at him, and doing your part (Hebrews 12:2). Examples of those with rugged faith: 1. Meshack, Shedrach, and Abednego: "Even if our God does not deliver us, we shall not bow to your idol" (Daniel 3:16-18, Daniel 3:25-26). 2. Esther: Standing in the gap for her people, "If I perish I perish" (Esther 4:16). 3. Paul: Ready to die for the gospel (2 Timothy 4:6-8). 4. Joseph: Ready to go to prison than sin against God (Genesis 39:9). 5. Abraham: God instructed him to sacrifice his only son. He did not argue with God (Genesis 22:2). 6. Job: Despite the loss of earthly possessions and children and provocation by the wife, Job maintained his integrity in the Lord (Job 19:25).

WHAT TO DO

1. Do not fret: the longer the journey seems, the closer your way home (Psalms 37:1). 2. Always remember, the back has no protection,

keep thrusting forward (Exodus 14:14-15). 4. Keep looking at the perfect law (the Word of God) of liberty that will set free (James 1:25). 5. Be fully armed with the weapons of warfare (Ephesians 6:11-13). 6. Keep praising and trusting God in all situations (Psalms 34:1).

Prayer points

- Father God, thank You because You alone are my guiding light.
- Father God, let my eyes be steady on You no matter the challenges of life.
- Father God, whatever will make me deny You, Father take it far from me.
- Father God, every obstacle, and distraction on this journey, please give me the grace to overcome.
- Father God, please have pleasure in me now and always, for I am the apple of Your eyes.
- Father God, having come this far, don't let me be a castaway in the long run.

In Jesus Name, Amen

Day 22
It Is Not Time to Wash Your Nets

And saw two ships standing by the lake: but the fishermen were gone out of them, and were washing their nets.
- Luke 5:2

Dearly beloved, have you ever got to a stage where you felt like throwing in the towel when it seemed to you that all your best efforts yielded no positive results and you felt like a fish out of water? Are you confused and unsure of yourself worth and capabilities and possibly looked like a first class failure? Welcome to Peter's Company (Luke 5:1-10). Do not give up there is still hope for you, joy comes in the morning (Job 14:7-9). Peter and his colleagues were in that very state of despair and frustration, toiling all night and never making a catch. Their story changed when Jesus entered the scene. It is so easy to get discouraged in the journey of life, but when you offer Jesus your shiplike Peter did, He will tell you where to cast your nets for a very big catch beyond your imaginations. Examples: 1. Rachel: Fruitless efforts or barrenness, she threatened suicide (Genesis 30:12). 2. Demas: Worldliness or Compromise: he loved the world more than Ministry (2 Timothy 4:10). 3. Elijah: Threats from the enemy; he requested to die instead of facing the enemy (1 Kings 19:1-4).

WHAT TO DO

1. Stop relying on your efforts, trust absolutely in the Lord (Proverbs 3:5-7). 2. Ask the Lord for fruitfulness and enlargement (1 Chronicles 4:9-10). 3. Confront the enemy in the name of the Lord (1 Samuel 17:45-50).

Prayer Points

- Father God, please put an end to all fruitless efforts in my life and give me boldness.
- Father God, please pilot the ship of my life, You are my anchor, don't let me sink.
- Father God, help me to keep hope alive, my best is on the way.
- Father God, please open a new chapter of joy, peace, and fulfillment in my life.

In Jesus Name, Amen

Day 23
Safeguard Your Good Name

A good name is rather to be chosen than great riches, and loving favour rather than silver and gold." Proverbs 22:1

In the olden days, when a young man was about to leave the village for the big city or going to another town for further academic pursuit, it was common to hear the parent say "remember the son of whom you are, please protect the good name of our family." Dearly beloved, the Word of God is reminding us that the choice of a good name far outweighs monetary and material values. Why was this so? Names to a large extent are pointers to destinies: 1. God has to change Abram (Exalted Father) to Abraham (Father of Multitudes) (Genesis 17:5). God made sure he became Father of Nations. 2. He changed Jacob (sup planter) to Israel (God prevails) (Genesis 32:28). Israel up till now prevails against all enemies around her. 3. Jesus renamed Simon (Listen) and called him Peter(The rock)-Matthew 16:18. Peter after repentance from his betrayal of Christ, became the foundational rock of the Apostolic movement (Acts 3:6). 4. Saul (the son I asked for) had his name changed to Paul (humble) -Acts 13:9. In spite of the chains of degrees Paul had, he humbled himself and made all his achievements dung for Christ (Philippians 3:8). 5. YOU: What is your name? What does it mean? How has it affected your destiny? Here is what God says about you: "Thou shalt no more be termed Forsaken; neither shall thy land any more be termed Desolate: but thou shalt be called Hephzibah, and thy land Beulah: for the Lord delighteth in thee, and thy land shall be married" (Isaiah 62:4). "But ye are a chosen generation, a royal priesthood, an holy nation, a peculiar people; that ye should shew forth the praises of him who hath called you out of darkness into his marvelous light:" (1 Peter 2:9).

WHAT TO DO

1. If your name negatively affects your destiny, ask God to change your name. 2. Call on the greatest name on earth - Jesus Christ - to swallow your name. 3. Call yourself by what God calls you. 4. Take the name of Jesus with you wherever you go. It is the name above all names (Philippians 2:9-10).

Prayer Points

- Father God, thank You that I am wonderfully and beautifully formed, and You know me before I was born.

- Father God, You changed Jabez (sorrowful) to someone greater than his brothers, please change my name for the better.

- Father God, let my name and those of our generation not be taken away from the Book of Life.

- Father God, our country is a land flowing with milk and honey, please restore our great name.

In Jesus Name, Amen

Day 24
Triumphing Over Tragedies

And having spoiled principalities and powers, he made a shew of them openly, triumphing over them in it.
- Colossians 2:15

Dearly beloved, we go through different trials and challenges in life. No man will escape trials but our response during and after matters a lot. Jesus commands us to be of good cheer. "These things I have spoken unto you, that in me ye might have peace. In the world ye shall have tribulation: but be of good cheer; I have overcome the world" (John 16:33). Are you going through very disturbing aspects of your life and it seems you are about to sink? Hope in the Lord, you will yet praise Him, and your joy shall be full. Read: Psalms 42:5, Psalms 71:5, Job 14:7. Examples: 1. Job: Despite all his losses he still affirmed his faith in Jehovah, "I know my Redeemer liveth" (Job 19:25). Results: God turned things around for him, and he lived gloriously thereafter (Job 42:10). 2. Apostle Paul: As a prisoner, suffered a devastating shipwreck on the way to Rome, God presence was an assurance for him (Acts 27: 22-25). 3. David: When he was terribly and ferociously hunted by King Saul in the wilderness, but David triumphed (Psalms 3:7). 4. YOU: What are you going through that is threatening your destiny and existence? God is no respecter of persons; He will do the same for you, just have faith in Him (Mark 11:22).

WHAT TO DO

1. Praise Him still in that situation. 2. Listen to His voice and obey Him. 3. Fret not thyself, just relax and let Him lead you (Psalms 37:7). 4. Be acquainted with Him so you can have peace (Job 22:21).

Prayer Points

- Father God, please shield me from the storms of life.
- Father God, no matter what comes my way, see me through and let it work for my good.
- Father God, I desire to hear your voice loud and clear as I go through life I am listening.
- Father God, I pray for my family, fight, for us, so we don't become casualties in the journey of life.

In Jesus Name, Amen

Day 25
The Doors of Freedom

And the Egyptians were urgent upon the people, that they might send them out of the land in haste; for they said, we be all dead men.
- Exodus 12:33

Dearly beloved, a door is very important to a building; they are fixed to make sure unwanted guests are not allowed in, if the door is locked, it can also prevent those inside from going out. All that the enemies and oppressors of your life have stolen shall be restored in the mighty name of Jesus (Joel 2:25-26). Every shut door shall be opened unto you, and your joy shall be full (John 16:24). In Exodus 12:33-36, it was the Passover meal that the children of Israel took that opened the door to freedom as they observed the strict instructions God gave them. They were delivered from oppression and servitude of 430 years. It doesn't matter for how long you have been in bondage; the Lord's meal will make a difference for you. It will open your closed womb. Examples: 1.Abraham and Sarah: The meal prepared by Abraham for his guests open the series of events that led to Sarah giving birth to Isaac (Genesis 18:12-14). 2. Shunamite Woman: Her fruitfulness started with her offer of a meal to the man of God, Elisha (2 Kings 4:8-17). 3. Peter: After Christ died, Peter went back to fishing with his colleagues, and he labored in vain like he did earlier in life. Soon Jesus had a mealwith them, and Peter never failed again (Luke 5:1-7; John 21:1-19).

WHAT TO DO

1. Align with the Lord and dine with Him. 2. Love what God loves, and hate what He hates. 3. Desire His presence and communion always. 4. Never take the body and blood of Jesus for granted.

Prayer Points

- Father God, please open my womb today, let me bring forth the precious gifts you have promised me.

- Father God, from today, as I dine with you, let every closed door be opened.

- Father God, let me never know failure again, physically, biologically, business, etc.

- Father God, close the door against the enemy and his agents.

- Father God, let the blood of Jesus prevail for me and be my defense.

- Father God, from now on, don't let me know poverty nor lack; as I am set free, give me beauty for my ashes.

In Jesus Name, Amen

Day 26
Move Forward

Remember ye not the former things, nor consider the things of old, behold I will do a new thing and it shall spring forth shall ye not know it? I will make ways..."
- Isaiah 43:18-19

Take your journey and move forward don't look back (Deuteronomy 1:6-7, Genesis 19:26). Yesterday is gone, and no matter how much you think about it, you cannot bring it back. Please understand that the past is a place of reference and not a place of residence. It is a sunk experience that should not drag you down. It is only the Almighty God that can go into your past and mercifully restructure your life so that the effects of the errors or mistakes of the past can be minimized or annulled. Dear Brethren, what you are today is a product of what you did yesterday and what you will become tomorrow is being fashioned out by what you are doing today. Dwelling on the success of yesterday might also stiffen the zeal to surpass records, and lead to complacency, conversely also, dwelling on the errors of the past results in these harmful habits: worry, regrets, frustration depression and weariness of body, soul, and spirit. Whichever way it is, yesterday is gone. Trust the Lord that henceforth, anything you do will be guided by the Lord (Psalms 32:8). Dearly Beloved, one fact stands above all else: The Lord wants the very best for His children no matter the rough terrain you have walked (3 John 2). He even went further to assure you of full restoration; please do not struggle with your Maker any more (Joel 2:25-26). Examples: Joseph, David, and Paul never allowed their pasts to define their future.

WHAT TO DO

1. Deliberately ask the Lord to help you forget the hurtful past after asking for forgiveness, move on.

2. Instead of worrying, start praising and worshipping the Lord like Paul and Silas did. 3. Start each new day asking the Lord for the program He has for you and follow it. 4. Cut away from things, places and people that easily remind you of the hurtful past, and that can take you back to it.

Prayer Points

- Father God, I am grateful that you understand and can deal with my past, present and future, please take me on in.

- Father God, please restructure my life and bring me joy once more.

- Father God, please do a complete makeover in my life and restore me totally.

- Father God, I ask for grace never to go back to those past and painful issues again.

- Father God, from now on, I yield myself as the clay in your hands; do to me as you please.

In Jesus Name, Amen

Day 27
The Paths of Righteousness

He restoreth my soul: he leadeth me in the paths of righteousness for his name's sake.
- Psalms 23:3

Dearly beloved, where are you on this journey of life? Are you at a cross-road or in a valley of decision? God not only encourages all us along godly paths but also specifically guides us along what He alone knows is the best of many possible straight paths? (Psalms 32:8; Hebrews 13:5b). Our human righteousness is as filthy rags and must be subordinate to Christ's righteousness for it to be acceptable to God (Isaiah 64:6; Romans 3:22). Examples of people adjudged as righteous: 1. Enoch: He had deep fellowship with God and God took him (Genesis 5:24). 2. Abraham: He had an unwavering faith in God and even obeyed God unreservedly (Galatians 3:6; Romans 4:16-20). 3. Noah: His obedience to the Lord in the face of undeniable odds, earned him a righteous disposition before God Almighty (Genesis 7:1, Romans 1:17). 4. Job: Stripped of all human and earthly possession, Job affirmed his faith in the supremacy of the Most High (Job 19:25). 5. Paul: Coming from a "hate" background became an outstanding lover and Apostle of the Lord Jesus Christ (1 Corinthians 15:10).6. YOU: Where do you stand on the "Scale of Righteousness"? Ok? or found wanting? (Micah 6:8).

WHAT TO DO

What are some steps to righteousness? 1. Seek and set your affection on heavenly things, and make God and His Kingdom your priority (Colossians 3:1-3; Matthew 6:33). 2. Be dead to sin and its appendages (Colossians 3:5; Ephesians 5:11). 3. Obey the Lord absolutely (Proverbs 3:5-6; Leviticus 20:26).

4. Put on Christ and the fullness of the Holy Spirit (Colossians 3:12-14; Ephesians 5:18). 5. Love what God loves, and hate what He hates (Hebrews 1:9, 1 Peter 2:21).

Prayer Points

- Father God, thank You for choosing to bless me by making me special.

- Father God, please let my path shine brighter still till the coming of the day.

- Father God, help me to make seeking Your Kingdom and righteousness a priority in my life.

- Father God, from now on, let my focus remain consistently on You alone.

- Father God, let nothing matter to me than doing Your will, and nothing but Your will.

In Jesus Name, Amen

Day 28
A New and Better Beginning

Beloved, I wish above all things that thou mayest prosper and be in health, even as thy soul prospereth.
- 3 John 1:2

Read: Isaiah 43:15-20. Dearly Beloved, welcome to a brand new day! The God of another chance will come through for you and your family in Jesus name, Amen. Two mighty forces determine how far and how great you can become in life and the other way round; each needs your cooperation for you to get there. Jesus came to give abundant life, and the devil came to give death ultimately (1 John 3:8). "The thief cometh not, but for to steal, and to kill, and to destroy: I am come that they might have life, and that they might have it more abundantly" (John 10:10). Let's consider some questions that make life worth living as you begin this new day: 1.Who do I love, and what am I doing about it? "Thou shalt love the Lord thy God…" (Deuteronomy 6:5; Matthew 6:33). 2. Am I pursuing my dream, or is fear stopping me, what is your vision? (Habakkuk. 2:2-4; Daniel 11:32b) 3. Am I adding value to life? "One thing have I desired of the Lord..."(Psalms 27:4). 4. What am I doing to help others?...reach out in love with the gospel and also give (Matthew 28:19-20; Luke 6:38). 5. Am I as good a person as I want to be? "That I might know Him...and be like Him..."

(Philippians 3:10; 1 John 3:2). Examples of those who lived & finished well: 1. Abraham...believed until the very end. 2. Enoch...he walked with God and was not ashamed. 3. David...he died fulfilled as a man after God. 4. Stephen, he died a martyr, gazing to heaven and praying for forgiveness for his murderers. 5. Paul, he finished gallantly and gloriously.

WHAT TO DO

1. Seek the Lord early and hold tight to Him. 2. Love what He loves & hate what He hates. 3. Obey Him completely and praise Him. 4. Pursue heavenly vision, and run with the end in mind. 5. Don't settle for less no matter what.

Prayer Points

- Father God, thank you for this new day, please help me till the end and beyond.
- Father God, please let me make full proof of my calling and pilgrimage.
- Father God, uphold my destiny in the hollow of your hands.
- Father God of another chance if I have missed it, help me retrace my steps and never to roam again.
- Father God, give me a new beginning.
- Father God, let my latter end be greater than my former.

In Jesus Name, Amen

Day 29
Unlocking the Doors of Your Destiny

And they come to Jesus, and see him that was possessed with the devil, and had the legion, sitting, and clothed, and in his right mind: and they were afraid.
- Mark 5:15

Dearly beloved, every life is created for a purpose. No life came into this world by accident. God is too busy to create a man without purpose, and God's purpose is a good one (Jeremiah 29:11). Even the mad man of Gadara, got his destiny restored at an encounter with Jesus (Mark 5:1-15). God will unlock the doors of your destiny in Jesus mighty name, Amen; your destiny shall not be aborted in Jesus name. Examples: 1. Jeremiah: He was born for a purpose. God ordained Him a prophet to the nation while in the womb (Jeremiah 1:4-5). 2. Jesus: came for a purpose; to destroy the works of the devil, and to give eternal life (1 John 3:8; John 10:10b). Jesus came to reverse all the doors the enemy has shut against you. 3. Gehazi: He had a defined destiny; with tutelage under Elisha but got his destiny aborted because of greed (2 Kings 5:26-27). 4. Methuselah: He lived for 969 years, and all he did was to beget sons and daughters, no serious tangible transferable nor sustainable impact, what a wasted destiny (Genesis 5:25-27). 5. Paul: He discovered purpose, ran with It, and finished strong (2 Timothy 4:7-8). If your destiny is correct, certain things will get manifested; here are some: 1. Everyone who is on course of his destiny will become a shining light (Matthew. 5:14; Proverb 4:18). 2. You begin to walk in dominion, like Elisha (Genesis1:28; James 5:17-18). 3.You become a man of impact like Jacob in the house of Laban (Genesis 12:2). 4. Any one fulfilling destiny will be a blessing. Jesus is a blessing to man kind (Acts 10:38). 5. David: Transformed 400 boys into mighty men of war (1 Samuel 22:1-2; 2 Samuel 10:7).

WHAT TO DO

To open and enter into your doors of destiny: 1. Believe in the Lord Jesus Christ (John 1:1, 12). 2.You must walk in righteousness (Hebrews 1:9). 3. Picture your future with the scriptures (Acts 20:32). 4. Make a violent demand for your destiny (1 Chronicles 4:9-10, Matthew 11:12). 5. Be a true Ambassador of the Lord (2 Corinthians 5:20).

Prayer Points

- Father God, don't let me pass through this world without discovering my destiny. I don't want to belong to a wasted generation

- Father God, the destiny of my family shall not be aborted; You will burst open all closed doors.

- Father God, for every waster of destiny in my life, my God arise and frustrate such.

- Father God, may my light shall shine for the world to see; no more obscurity.

- Father God, from today, the embargo over my life, family, and ministry are lifted.

In Jesus Name, Amen

Day 30
Soar like The Eagle, Fly Eagle Fly

But they that wait upon the Lord shall renew their strength; they shall mount up with wings as eagles; they shall run, and not be weary, and they shall walk, and not faint.
- Isaiah 40:30

Dearly beloved when God created you, He looked at you and said "this is very good" remember you are the apple of God's eyes and you are fearfully and wonderfully made (Genesis 1:26-31). You were created to exercise dominion because God wants the best for you (Jeremiah 29:11). "Thou shall be head and not the tail, above only and not beneath" (Deuteronomy 28:13a). Friend, you are a peculiar person; don't settle for less, arise and take your rightful place above challenging situations of life. You are worth much more than you think or imagine. You are not a chicken; you are an eagle. Mount up with your wings and soar high and reach greater heights. Are you already playing second fiddle in your home, ministry or business? Don't settle for less, you are the best, and remain the best. Yes, don't let the devil give you that inferiority dummy any longer. Remember, Jabez refused to settle for less; he cried to the Lord despite the curse placed upon him by his mother, the Lord answered all his requests, he became more honorable than his brethren (1 Chronicles 4:9-10). It is your turn, therefore, arise and soar. Fly Eagle Fly!!!

WHAT TO DO

1. Push for excellence (Proverbs 22:29). 2. Pursue your Godgiven vision (Habakkuk 3:1-4). 3. Reposition yourself for greatness. 4. Believe you can achieve your dreams (Luke 1:37; Philippians 4:13). 5.

Ignite and activate your potentials and improve on a continuous basis (1 Corinthians 15:58).

Prayer Points

- Father God, thank you for making me who I am, let me be the best in all areas of my life.

- Father God, give me the grace to drop every weight pulling me down.

- Father God, let me rise above any limitation to my growth, development, and destiny.

- Father God, release me from any captivity of servitude: and let me enter into my destiny.

- Father God, please take me to the mountaintop and make me reign.

In Jesus Name, Amen

About the Author

Hello, **I am Prophetess Reverend Rita Monique Henderson**, I am a 2x Best Selling Author, Speaker, Clarity Coach and Spiritual Midwife.

I have led many to birth their God-ordained purpose by my unique style of preaching, workshops, mentorship program, and Each One Reach One Mini Bible Study Correspondence Courses.

On a Monday in 2011, the Lord called me off what I called my good government job after working 28 years. As I was driving home, from work, the Lord said: "When you drive away from here today, daughter, don't you ever drive back here again. And I promise you that if you will take care of my business, I will take care of all of your business." I can tell you that I never drove back there and why, because, YOU - Beloved, is His business.

He has purposed me to guide you to DISCOVER, DEFINE, DEMONSTRATE and DOMINATE your God-ordained purpose.

Understand that operating in your purpose will bring you the prosperity in which God promises, for it is the road of purpose that leads to prosperity.

My programs can help you to:

Discover your natural talents and gain confidence.

Tap into your highest potential and define your true purpose.

Gain the results you long for, and prosper.

If you are ready to move from a place of defeat to a place of destiny join my private FB Community Monetize Ministry with Reverend Rita, Your Passion, Your Purpose, Your Profits! @ bit.ly/purposetoprosper.

God bless you richly.

Reverend Rita

Connect with Reverend Rita

Email: reverendrita@monetizeyourministry.org

Enhance your experience purchase the 30 Day companion journal - Increased Faith Journal at monetizeyourministry.org

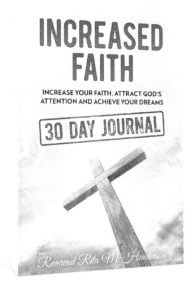

Made in the
USA
Middletown, DE